Sense of Taste

Carey Molter

WOOSTER LOWER SCHOOL

Published by SandCastle™, an imprint of ABDO Publishing Company, 4940 Viking Drive, Edina, Minnesota 55435.

Printed in the United States.

Photo credits: Corbis Images, Corel, Image 100, PhotoDisc, Stockbyte

Library of Congress Cataloging-in-Publication Data

Molter, Carey, 1973-
    Sense of taste / Carey Molter.
        p. cm. -- (The senses)
    Includes index.
    ISBN 1-57765-629-6
        1. Taste--Juvenile literature. [1. Taste. 2. Senses and sensation.] I. Title.

QP456 .M64 2001
612.8'7--dc21

2001022904

The SandCastle concept, content, and reading method have been reviewed and approved by a national advisory board including literacy specialists, librarians, elementary school teachers, early childhood education professionals, and parents.

Let Us Know

After reading the book, SandCastle would like you to tell us your stories about reading. What is your favorite page? Was there something hard that you needed help with? Share the ups and downs of learning to read. We want to hear from you! To get posted on the Abdo Publishing Company Web site, send us email at:

sandcastle@abdopub.com

About SandCastle™
Nonfiction books for the beginning reader

- Basic concepts of phonics are incorporated with integrated language methods of reading instruction. Most words are short, and phrases, letter sounds, and word sounds are repeated.

- Readability is determined by the number of words in each sentence, the number of characters in each word, and word lists based on curriculum frameworks.

- Full-color photography reinforces word meanings and concepts.

- "Words I Can Read" list at the end of each book teaches basic elements of grammar, helps the reader recognize the words in the text, and builds vocabulary.

- Reading levels are indicated by the number of flags on the castle.

Note: Some pages in this book contain more than ten words in order to more clearly convey the concept of the book.

Look for more SandCastle books in these three reading levels:

Level 1 (one flag)	**Level 2** (two flags)	**Level 3** (three flags)

Grades Pre-K to K 5 or fewer words per page	**Grades K to 1** 5 to 10 words per page	**Grades 1 to 2** 10 to 15 words per page

Our senses tell us what
is happening around us.

Taste is one of our five senses.

Taste is how we know
what is in our mouths.

Sweet foods and drinks taste like sugar.

Candy is sweet.

Some things have no taste.

Carl likes plain water.

Some food tastes salty.

Robert likes salty snacks.

Sour things have a sharp taste.

Lemonade can taste sour.

Drinks that are not
sweet taste bitter.

Iced tea tastes bitter.

Anna has a treat.

How do you think it tastes?

Words I Can Read

Nouns

A noun is a person, place, or thing

candy (KAN-dee) p. 11

food (FOOD) p. 15

iced tea
(EYESST TEE) p. 19

lemonade
(lem-uh-NADE) p. 17

sugar (SHUG-ur) p. 11

taste
(TAYST) pp. 7, 9, 13, 17

treat (TREET) p. 21

water (WAW-tur) p. 13

Plural Nouns

**A plural noun is more than one
person, place, or thing**

drinks
(DRINGKSS) pp. 11, 19

foods (FOODZ) p. 11

mouths (MOUTHZ) p. 9

senses
(SENSS-ez) pp. 5, 7

snacks (SNAKSS) p. 15

things
(THINGZ) pp. 9, 13, 17

Proper Nouns

**A proper noun is the name
of a person, place, or thing**

Anna (AN-uh) p. 21

Carl (KARL) p. 13

Robert (ROB-urt) p. 15

Verbs
A verb is an action or being word

are (AR) p. 19

can (KAN) p. 17

do (DOO) p. 21

happening
  (HAP-uhn-ing) p. 5

has (HAZ) p. 21

have (HAV) pp. 13, 17

is (IZ) pp. 5, 7, 9, 11

know (NOH) p. 9

likes (LIKESS) pp. 13, 15

taste (TAYST)
  pp. 11, 17, 19

tastes (TAYSTSS)
  pp. 15, 19, 21

tell (TEL) p. 5

think (THINGK) p. 21

Adjectives
An adjective describes something

bitter (BIT-ur) p. 19

five (FIVE) p. 7

no (NOH) p. 13

one (WUHN) p. 7

plain (PLANE) p. 13

salty (SAWLT-ee) p. 15

sharp (SHARP) p. 17

some (SUHM) pp. 13, 15

sour (SOUR) p. 17

sweet
  (SWEET) pp. 11, 19

More About the Sense of Taste
Match the Words to their Pictures

tart

spicy

taste buds

minty

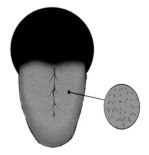